Dear

Dear Love

Also from Charles McEnerney & Adam Larson:

Dear Graduate

A book for when we take a step forward.

Dear Love

A book about being together.

Charles McEnerney & Adam Larson

Clarkson Potter/Publishers
New York

Clarkson Potter/Publishers
An imprint of the Crown Publishing Group
A division of Penguin Random House LLC
1745 Broadway
New York, NY 10019
clarksonpotter.com
penguinrandomhouse.com

Library of Congress Cataloging-in-Publication Data is on file with the publisher.

ISBN 979-8-217-03532-8
Ebook ISBN 979-8-217-03533-5

Editor: Emma Brodie | Assistant editor: Bri James
Designer: Adam Larson | Art director: Ian Dingman
Production editor: Leni Schenkel | Production: Jessica Heim

Manufactured in China

10 9 8 7 6 5 4 3 2 1

First Edition

The authorized representative in the EU for product safety and compliance is Penguin Random House Ireland, Morrison Chambers, 32 Nassau Street, Dublin D02 YH68, Ireland, https://eu-contact.penguin.ie.

For bubba, for helping
me become a better
version of myself

I wanted to get
you something
to show you
how I feel.

But what *thing* could possibly do that?

I thought and
looked and swiped
and scrolled.
Nothing was
quite right.

So, I decided to give you some ideas to choose from instead.

Now that you have chosen me and I have chosen you...

I think about you all the time, and there is so much I want to do together.

So, let's go to
a small town
and spend the
day in bookstores
and cafés and
movie theaters.

Let's browse shops with antiques, vinyl, and everything old and new.

Let's take a stroll in the park, hike in the woods, or trek up a trail.

Let's spend
an afternoon
picking berries,
apples, pumpkins,
or flowers.

Let's go to the
beach, chase
the waves,
watch seagulls,
and hunt for
beautiful shells.

Let's lie in a river
or dawdle on a
dock, kayak on
a lake or sail
across the sea.

Let's bike to new places, discover new restaurants, and turn strangers into friends.

Let's meander winding roads, through hills and valleys, into the unknown.

Let's go to a brewery, winery, distillery, or juicery.

Let's eat takeout
on the couch and
watch something
that makes us laugh.

Let’s go to a carnival, music festival, or a fair.

Let's wander galleries and museums, and be inspired by art in all its forms.

Let’s take a walk through falling leaves, while it snows, or as the wind blows and flowers sway.

Let's go to the gym, out for a run, or for a relaxing swim.

Let's explore far-off places, to see, smell, hear, taste, and experience the unfamiliar.

Let's watch the sun rise, see the sun set, or look for the moon and planets in the sky.

Let's practice meditation, yoga, or tai chi and be side-by-side in mind and body.

Let's plant seeds or bulbs and help them to grow.

Let's find a recipe we've never tried and make a delicious meal together.

Let's help each other wash the dishes, clean the clothes, and sweep the floors.

Let's listen to
our favorite music
and dance the
night away.

Let's lie in bed all
day, reading for
hours and hours
and hours
and hours
and hours
and hours

Let's create together, make bread, make art, or make love.

Let's hold hands everywhere we possibly can.

Let's kiss in the rain, in the fog, and beneath the falling stars.

Let's take the road less traveled and get lost for a while.

Let's keep our ears and minds open, so we can always hear and understand each other.

Let me tell you,
"I love you."

And take a pause
to really hear it.

Let's be grateful for one another and look forward to looking back at these times.

Moments will
come and go,
but our love will
forever be ours.

Let’s remember that
time is precious.

And whatever we do, let's be here now.

Because now
is always better
when I'm with you.

Charles McEnerney

Charles McEnerney is a writer, musician, marketer and, most importantly, a dad to Adacie and Declan. He is the co-author of *Dear Graduate*. Throughout his career, he has worked at HBO, GBH/PBS, *Fast Company*, *Inc.*, and *MovieMaker* magazines, Emerson College, The Grommet, and 826 Boston. Charlie was the singer/songwriter in the post-punk band Falling Stairs and is now a solo artist. Charlie grew up in Flushing, Queens, and lives in Jamaica Plain in Boston, MA. If he's not writing, he is likely listening to music, playing music, reading, watching the news, or with Adam in some small-town bookstore looking for a book he doesn't have room for at home. **charlesmcenerney.com**

Adam Larson

Adam Larson is an award-winning creative director, designer, artist, and illustrator. He is the co-author of *Dear Graduate*. He is the founder of the multidisciplinary brand design studio Adam&Co., whose clients have included Beyoncé, Taylor Swift, Herbie Hancock, Hoka, Nike, Puma, Saucony, Converse, The Boston Public Library, Harvard, NYU, MIT, CNN, ESPN, Penguin Books, and Random House, among others. He is the co-founding editor and art director of *Lemon* and *Wednesday* magazines. He has taught design at MassArt and currently lives in Florence, MA. If he's not doting on his American Bully, Rhys, he is likely reading; at a gallery, museum, or bookstore; or riding his bike with Charlie down Commercial Street in Provincetown. **adamnco.com**

Thank You

Emma Brodie at Clarkson Potter,
Kristin van Ogtrop at InkWell Management,
Barbara Daly, Natalie Jackvony, Adacie McEnerney, Declan McEnerney,
Carlos Prieto, Marion Seymour, and Jacqui Turpin,
for all of your support.

And thank you to all of the bookstores and gift shops
that carried our first book, *Dear Graduate*!